Abraham Lincoln

A Play

John Drinkwater

HAWK PRESS

Published by

Hawk Press
4836/24, Ansari Road, Daryaganj
New Delhi – 110 002
Phones : 9643330713, +91-11-23278618, +91-11-35676207
E-mail: thehawkpress@gmail.com
www.thehawkpress.com

ISBN : 978-93-92322-74-7

NOTE

In using for purposes of drama a personality of so wide and recent a fame as that of Abraham Lincoln, I feel that one or two observations are due to my readers and critics.

First, my purpose is that not of the historian but of the dramatist. The historical presentation of my hero has been faithfully made in many volumes; notably, in England, by Lord Charnwood in a monograph that gives a masterly analysis of Lincoln's career and character and is, it seems to me, a model of what the historian's work should be. To this book I am gratefully indebted for the material of my play. But while I have, I hope, done nothing to traverse history, I have freely telescoped its events, and imposed invention upon its movement, in such ways as I needed to shape the dramatic significance of my subject. I should add that the fictitious Burnet Hook is admitted to the historical company of Lincoln's Cabinet for the purpose of embodying certain forces that were antagonistic to the President. This was a dramatic necessity, and I chose rather to invent a character for the purpose than to invest any single known personage with sinister qualities about which there might be dispute.

Secondly, my purpose is, again, that of the dramatist, not that of the political philosopher. The issue of secession was a very intricate one, upon which high and generous opinions may be in conflict, but that I may happen to have or lack personal sympathy with Lincoln's policy and judgment in this matter is nothing. My concern is with the profoundly dramatic interest of his character, and with the inspiring example of a man who handled war nobly and with imagination.

Finally, I am an Englishman, and not a citizen of the great country that gave Lincoln birth. I have, therefore, written as an Englishman, making no attempt to achieve a "local colour" of which I have no experience, or to speak in an idiom to which I have not been bred. To have done otherwise, as I am sure any American friends that this play may have the good fortune to make will allow, would have been to treat a great subject with levity.

J.D.

Far Oakridge, July-August, 1918

INTRODUCTORY NOTE

This play was originally produced by the Birmingham Repertory Theatre last year, and it had a great success in Birmingham. But if its author had not happened to be the artistic director of the Birmingham Repertory Theatre the play might never have been produced there. The rumour of the provincial success reached London, with the usual result—that London managers magnificently ignored it. I have myself spoken with a very well-known London actor-manager who admitted to me that he had refused the play.

When Nigel Playfair, in conjunction with myself as a sort of Chancellor of the Exchequer, started the Hammersmith Playhouse (for the presentation of the best plays that could be got) we at once began to inquire into the case of Abraham Lincoln. Nigel Playfair was absolutely determined to have the play and the Birmingham company to act it. I read the play and greatly admired it. We secured both the play and the company. The first Hammersmith performance was a tremendous success, both for the author of the play and for William J. Rea, the Irish actor who in the rôle of Lincoln was merely great. The audience cried.

I should have cried myself, but for my iron resolve not to stain a well-earned reputation for callousness. As I returned home that night from what are known as "the wilds of Hammersmith" (Hammersmith is a suburb of London) I said to myself: "This play is bound to succeed" The next moment I said to myself: "This play cannot possibly succeed. It has no love interest. It is a political play. Its theme is the threatened separation of the Southern States from the Northern States. Nobody ever heard of a play with such an absurd theme reaching permanent success. No author before John Drinkwater ever had the effrontery to impose such a theme on a London public."

My instinct was right and my reason was wrong. The play did

succeed. It is still succeeding, and it will continue to succeed. Nobody can dine out in London to-day and admit without a blush that he has not seen Abraham Lincoln. Monarchs and princes have seen it. Archbishops have seen it. Statesmen without number have seen it. An ex-Lord Chancellor told me that he had journeyed out into the said wilds and was informed at the theatre that there were no seats left. He could not believe that he would have to return from the wilds unsatisfied. But so it fell out. West End managers have tried to coax the play from Hammersmith to the West End. They could not do it. We have contrived to make all London come to Hammersmith to see a play without a love-interest or a bedroom scene, and the play will remain at Hammersmith. Americans will more clearly realize what John Drinkwater has achieved with the London public if they imagine somebody putting on a play about the Crimean War at some unknown derelict theatre round about Two Hundred and Fiftieth Street, and drawing all New York to Two Hundred and Fiftieth Street.

Abraham Lincoln has pleased everybody, and its triumph is the best justification of those few who held that the public was capable of liking much better plays than were offered to the public. Why has Abraham Lincoln succeeded? Here are a few answers to the question: Because the author had a deep, practical knowledge of the stage. Because he disdained all stage tricks. Because he had the wit to select for his hero one of the world's greatest and finest characters. Because he had the audacity to select a gigantic theme and to handle it with simplicity. Because he had the courage of all his artistic and moral convictions. And of course because he has a genuine dramatic gift. Finally, because William J. Rea plays Lincoln with the utmost nobility of emotional power.

Every audience has the same experience at Abraham Lincoln, and I laugh privately when I think of that experience. The curtain goes up on a highly commonplace little parlour, and a few ordinary people chatting in a highly commonplace manner. They keep on chatting. The audience thinks to itself: "I've been done! What is this interminable small talk?" And it wants to call out a protest: "Hi! You fellows on the stage! Have you forgotten that there is an audience on the other side of the footlights, waiting for something to happen?" (Truly the ordinary people in the parlour do seem to be unaware of the existence of any audience.) But wait, audience! Already the author is winding his chains about you. Though you may not suspect it, you are already bound.... At the end of the first scene the audience, vaguely feeling the spell, wonders what on earth the nature of the spell is. At the end of the play it is perhaps still wondering what precisely the nature of the spell is.... But it fully and rapturously admits the reality of the spell. Indeed after the fall of the curtain, and after many falls of the curtain, the spell persists; the audience somehow cannot leave its seats, and the thought of the worry of the journey home and of last 'busses and trains is banished. Strange phenomenon! It occurs every night.

ARNOLD BENNETT
April 1919

Two Chroniclers:

The two speaking together: Kinsmen, you shall behold
Our stage, in mimic action, mould
A man's character.
This is the wonder, always, everywhere—
Not that vast mutability which is event,
The pits and pinnacles of change,
But man's desire and valiance that range
All circumstance, and come to port unspent.
Agents are these events, these ecstasies,
And tribulations, to prove the purities
Or poor oblivions that are our being. When
Beauty and peace possess us, they are none
But as they touch the beauty and peace of men,
Nor, when our days are done,
And the last utterance of doom must fall,
Is the doom anything
Memorable for its apparelling;
The bearing of man facing it is all.
So, kinsmen, we present
This for no loud event
That is but fugitive,
But that you may behold
Our mimic action mould
The spirit of man immortally to live.
First Chronicler: Once when a peril touched the days
Of freedom in our English ways,
And none renowned in government

Was equal found,
Came to the steadfast heart of one,
Who watched in lonely Huntingdon,
A summons, and he went,
And tyranny was bound,
And Cromwell was the lord of his event.
Second Chronicler: And in that land where voyaging
The pilgrim Mayflower came to rest,
Among the chosen, counselling,
Once, when bewilderment possessed
A people, none there was might draw
To fold the wandering thoughts of men,
And make as one the names again
Of liberty and law.
And then, from fifty fameless years
In quiet Illinois was sent
A word that still the Atlantic hears,
And Lincoln was the lord of his event.
The two speaking together: So the uncounted
spirit wakes
To the birth
Of uncounted circumstance.
And time in a generation makes
Portents majestic a little story of earth
To be remembered by chance
At a fireside.
But the ardours that they bear,
The proud and invincible motions of
character—
These—these abide.

SCENE I.

The parlour of Abraham Lincoln's House at Springfield, Illinois, early in 1860. MR. STONE, a farmer, and MR. CUFFNEY, a store-keeper, both men of between fifty and sixty, are sitting before an early spring fire. It is dusk, but the curtains are not drawn. The men are smoking silently.

Mr. Stone (after a pause): Abraham. It's a good name for a man to bear, anyway.

Mr. Cuffney: Yes. That's right.

Mr. Stone (after another pause): Abraham Lincoln. I've known him forty years. Never crooked once. Well.

He taps his pipe reflectively on the grate. There is another pause. SUSAN, a servant-maid, comes in, and busies herself lighting candles and drawing the curtains to.

Susan: Mrs. Lincoln has just come in. She says she'll be here directly.

Mr. Cuffney: Thank you.

Mr. Stone: Mr. Lincoln isn't home yet, I dare say?

Susan: No, Mr. Stone. He won't be long, with all the gentlemen coming.

Mr. Stone: How would you like your master to be President of the United States, Susan?

Susan: I'm sure he'd do it very nicely, sir.

Mr. Cuffney: He would have to leave Springfield, Susan, and go to live in Washington.

Susan: I dare say we should take to Washington very well, sir.

Mr. Cuffney: Ah! I'm glad to hear that.

Susan: Mrs. Lincoln's rather particular about the tobacco smoke.

Mr. Stone: To be sure, yes, thank you, Susan.

Susan: The master doesn't smoke, you know. And Mrs. Lincoln's specially particular about this room.

Mr. Cuffney: Quite so. That's very considerate of you, Susan.

They knock out their pipes.

Susan: Though some people might not hold with a gentleman not doing as he'd a mind in his own house, as you might say.

She goes out.

Mr. Cuffney (after a further pause, stroking his pipe): I suppose there's no doubt about the message they'll bring?

Mr. Stone: No, that's settled right enough. It'll be an invitation. That's as sure as John Brown's dead.

Mr. Cuffney: I could never make Abraham out rightly about old John. One couldn't stomach slaving more than the other, yet Abraham didn't hold with the old chap standing up against it with the sword. Bad philosophy, or something, he called it. Talked about fanatics who do nothing but get themselves at a rope's end.

Mr. Stone: Abraham's all for the Constitution. He wants the Constitution to be an honest master. There's nothing he wants like that, and he'll stand for that, firm as a Samson of the spirit, if he goes to Washington. He'd give his life to persuade the state against slaving, but until it is persuaded and makes its laws against it, he'll have nothing to do with violence in the name of laws that aren't made. That's why old John's raiding affair stuck in his gullet.

Mr. Cuffney: He was a brave man, going like that, with a few zealous like himself, and a handful of niggers, to free thousands.

Mr. Stone: He was. And those were brave words when they took him out to hang him. "I think, my friends, you are guilty of a great wrong against God and humanity. You may dispose of me very easily. I am nearly disposed of now. But this question is still to be settled—this negro question, I mean. The end of that is not yet." I was there that day. Stonewall Jackson was there. He turned away. There was a colonel there giving orders. When it was over, "So perish all foes of the human race," he called out. But only those that were afraid of losing their slaves believed it.

Mr. Cuffney (after a pause): It was a bad thing to hang a man like that. ... There's a song that they've made about him.

He sings quietly.

John Brown's body lies a mould'ring in the grave,
But his soul goes marching on...

Mr. Stone: I know.

The two together (singing quietly):

The stars of heaven are looking kindly down
On the grave of old John Brown....

After a moment MRS. LINCOLN comes in. The men rise.

Mrs. Lincoln: Good-evening, Mr. Stone. Good-evening, Mr. Cuffney.

Mr. Stone and Mr. Cuffney: Good-evening, ma'am.

Mrs. Lincoln: Sit down, if you please.

They all sit.

Mr. Stone: This is a great evening for you, ma'am.

Mrs. Lincoln: It is.

Mr. Cuffney: What time do you expect the deputation, ma'am?

Mrs. Lincoln: They should be here at seven o'clock. (With an inquisitive nose.) Surely, Abraham hasn't been smoking.

Mr. Stone (rising): Shall I open the window, ma'am? It gets close of an evening.

Mrs. Lincoln: Naturally, in March. You may leave the window, Samuel Stone. We do not smoke in the parlour.

Mr. Stone (resuming his seat): By no means, ma'am.

Mrs. Lincoln: I shall be obliged to you.

Mr. Cuffney: Has Abraham decided what he will say to the invitation?

Mrs. Lincoln: He will accept it.

Mr. Stone: A very right decision, if I may say so.

Mrs. Lincoln: It is.

Mr. Cuffney: And you, ma'am, have advised him that way, I'll be bound.

Mrs. Lincoln: You said this was a great evening for me. It is, and I'll say more than I mostly do, because it is. I'm likely to go into history now with a great man. For I know better than any how great he is. I'm plain looking and I've a sharp tongue, and I've a mind that doesn't always go in his easy, high way. And that's what history will see, and it will laugh a little, and say, "Poor Abraham Lincoln." That's all right, but it's not all. I've always known when he should go forward, and when he should hold back. I've watched, and watched, and what I've learnt America will profit by. There are women like that, lots of them. But I'm lucky. My work's going farther than Illinois—it's going farther than any of us can tell. I made things easy for him to think and think when we were poor, and now his thinking has brought him to this. They wanted to make him Governor of Oregon, and he would have gone and have come to nothing there. I stopped him. Now they're coming to ask him to be President, and I've told him to go.

Mr. Stone: If you please, ma'am, I should like to apologise for smoking in here.

Mrs. Lincoln: That's no matter, Samuel Stone. Only, don't do it again.

Mr. Cuffney: It's a great place for a man to fill. Do you know how Seward takes Abraham's nomination by the Republicans?

Mrs. Lincoln: Seward is ambitious. He expected the nomination. Abraham will know how to use him.

Mr. Stone: The split among the Democrats makes the election of the Republican choice a certainty, I suppose?

Mrs. Lincoln: Abraham says so.

Mr. Cuffney: You know, it's hard to believe. When I think of the times I've sat in this room of an evening, and seen your husband come in, ma'am, with his battered hat nigh falling off the back of his head, and stuffed with papers that won't go into his pockets, and god-darning some rascal who'd done him about an assignment or a trespass, I can't think he's going up there into the eyes of the world.

Mrs. Lincoln: I've tried for years to make him buy a new hat.

Mr. Cuffney: I have a very large selection just in from New York. Perhaps Abraham might allow me to offer him one for his departure.

Mrs. Lincoln: He might. But he'll wear the old one.

Mr. Stone: Slavery and the South. They're big things he'll have to deal with. "The end of that is not yet." That's what old John Brown said, "the end of that is not yet."

ABRAHAM LINCOLN comes in, a greenish and crumpled top hat leaving his forehead well uncovered, his wide pockets brimming over with documents. He is fifty, and he still preserves his clean-shaven state. He kisses his wife and shakes hands with his friends.

Lincoln: Well, Mary. How d'ye do, Samuel. How d'ye do, Timothy.

Mr. Stone and Mr. Cuffney: Good-evening, Abraham.

Lincoln (while he takes of his hat and shakes out sundry papers from the lining into a drawer): John Brown, did you say? Aye, John Brown. But that's not the way it's to be done. And you can't do the right thing the wrong way. That's as bad as the wrong thing, if you're going to keep the state together.

Mr. Cuffney: Well, we'll be going. We only came in to give you good-faring, so to say, in the great word you've got to speak this evening.

Mr. Stone: It makes a humble body almost afraid of himself, Abraham, to know his friend is to be one of the great ones of the earth, with his yes and no law for these many, many thousands of folk.

Lincoln: It makes a man humble to be chosen so, Samuel. So humble that no man but would say "No" to such bidding if he dare. To be President of this people, and trouble gathering everywhere in men's hearts. That's a searching thing. Bitterness, and scorn, and wrestling often with men I shall despise, and perhaps nothing truly done at the end. But I must go. Yes. Thank you, Samuel; thank you, Timothy. Just a glass of that cordial, Mary, before they leave.

He goes to a cupboard.

May the devil smudge that girl!

Calling at the door.

Susan! Susan Deddington! Where's that darnation cordial?

Mrs. Lincoln: It's all right, Abraham. I told the girl to keep it out. The cupboard's choked with papers.

Susan (coming in with bottle and glasses): I'm sure I'm sorry. I was told—

Lincoln: All right, all right, Susan. Get along with you.

Susan: Thank you, sir. She goes.

Lincoln (pouring out drink): Poor hospitality for whiskey-drinking rascals like yourselves. But the thought's good.

Mr. Stone: Don't mention it, Abraham.

Mr. Cuffney: We wish you well, Abraham. Our compliments, ma'am. And God bless America! Samuel, I give you the United States, and Abraham Lincoln.

MR. CUFFNEY and MR. STONE drink.

Mrs. Lincoln: Thank you.

Lincoln: Samuel, Timothy—I drink to the hope of honest friends. Mary, to friendship. I'll need that always, for I've a queer, anxious heart. And, God bless America!

He and MRS. LINCOLN drink.

Mr. Stone: Well, good-night, Abraham. Goodnight, ma'am.

Mr. Cuffney: Good-night, good-night.

Mrs. Lincoln: Good-night, Mr. Stone. Good-night, Mr. Cuffney.

Lincoln: Good-night, Samuel. Good-night, Timothy. And thank you for coming.

MR. STONE and MR. CUFFNEY go out.

Mrs. Lincoln: You'd better see them in here.

Lincoln: Good. Five minutes to seven. You're sure about it, Mary?

Mrs. Lincoln: Yes. Aren't you?

Lincoln: We mean to set bounds to slavery. The South will resist. They may try to break away from the Union. That cannot be allowed. If the Union is set aside America will crumble. The saving of it may mean blood.

Mrs. Lincoln: Who is to shape it all if you don't?

Lincoln: There's nobody. I know it.

Mrs. Lincoln: Then go.

Lincoln: Go.

Mrs. Lincoln (after a moment): This hat is a disgrace to you, Abraham. You pay no heed to what I say, and you think it doesn't matter. A man like you ought to think a little about gentility.

Lincoln: To be sure. I forget.

Mrs. Lincoln: You don't. You just don't heed. Samuel Stone's been smoking in here.

Lincoln: He's a careless, poor fellow.

Mrs. Lincoln: He is, and a fine example you set him. You don't care whether he makes my parlour smell poison or not.

Lincoln: Of course I do—

Mrs. Lincoln: You don't. Your head is too stuffed with things to think about my ways. I've got neighbours if you haven't.

Lincoln: Well, now, your neighbours are mine, I suppose.

Mrs. Lincoln: Then why won't you consider appearances a little?

Lincoln: Certainly. I must.

Mrs. Lincoln: Will you get a new hat?

Lincoln: Yes, I must see about it.

Mrs. Lincoln: When?

Lincoln: In a day or two. Before long.

Mrs. Lincoln: Abraham, I've got a better temper than anybody will ever guess.

Lincoln: You have, my dear. And you need it, I confess.

SUSAN comes in.

Susan: The gentlemen have come.

Mrs. Lincoln: I'll come to them.

Susan: Does the master want a handkerchief, ma'am? He didn't take one this morning.

Lincoln: It's no matter now, Susan.

Susan: If you please, I've brought you one, sir.

She gives it to him, and goes.

Mrs. Lincoln: I'll send them in. Abraham, I believe in you.

Lincoln: I know, I know.

MRS. LINCOLN goes out. LINCOLN moves to a map of the United States that is hanging on the wall, and stands silently looking at it. After a few moments SUSAN comes to the door.

Susan: This way, please.

She shows in WILLIAM TUCKER, a florid, prosperous merchant; HENRY HIND, an alert little attorney; ELIAS PRICE, a lean lay preacher; and JAMES MACINTOSH, the editor of a Republican journal. SUSAN goes.

Tucker: Mr. Lincoln. Tucker my name is—William Tucker.

He presents his companions.

Mr. Henry Hind—follows your profession, Mr. Lincoln. Leader of the bar in Ohio. Mr. Elias Price, of Pennsylvania. You've heard him preach, maybe. James Macintosh you know. I come from Chicago.

Lincoln: Gentlemen, at your service. How d'ye do, James. Will you be seated?

They sit round the table.

Tucker: I have the honour to be chairman of this delegation. We are sent from Chicago by the Republican Convention, to enquire whether you will accept their invitation to become the Republican candidate for the office of President of the United States.

Price: The Convention is aware, Mr. Lincoln, that under the circumstances, seeing that the Democrats have split, this is more than an invitation to candidature. Their nominee is almost certain to be elected.

Lincoln: Gentlemen, I am known to one of you only. Do you know my many disqualifications for this work?

Hind: It's only fair to say that they have been discussed freely.

Lincoln: There are some, shall we say graces, that I lack. Washington does not altogether neglect these.

Tucker: They have been spoken of. But these are days, Mr. Lincoln, if I may say so, too difficult, too dangerous, for these to weigh at the expense of other qualities that you were considered to possess.

Lincoln: Seward and Hook have both had great experience.

Macintosh: Hook had no strong support. For Seward, there are doubts as to his discretion.

Lincoln: Do not be under any misunderstanding, I beg you. I aim at moderation so far as it is honest. But I am a very stubborn man, gentlemen. If the South insists upon the extension of slavery, and claims the right to secede, as you know it very well may do, and the decision lies with me, it will mean resistance, inexorable, with blood if needs be. I would have everybody's mind clear as to that.

Price: It will be for you to decide, and we believe you to be an upright man, Mr. Lincoln.

Lincoln: Seward and Hook would be difficult to carry as subordinates.

Tucker: But they will have to be carried so, and there's none likelier for the job than you.

Lincoln: Will your Republican Press stand by me for a principle, James, whatever comes?

Macintosh: There's no other man we would follow so readily.

Lincoln: If you send me, the South will have little but derision for your choice.

Hind: We believe that you'll last out their laughter.

Lincoln: I can take any man's ridicule—I'm trained to it by a ... somewhat odd figure that it pleased God to give me, if I may so far be pleasant with you. But this slavery business will be long, and deep, and bitter. I know it. If you do me this honour, gentlemen, you must look to me for no compromise in this matter. If abolition comes in due time by constitutional means, good. I want it. But, while we will not force abolition, we will give slavery no approval, and we will not allow it to extend its boundaries by one yard. The determination is in my blood.

When I was a boy I made a trip to New Orleans, and there I saw them, chained, beaten, kicked as a man would be ashamed to kick a thieving dog. And I saw a young girl driven up and down the room that the bidders might satisfy themselves. And I said then, "If ever I get a chance to hit that thing, I'll hit it hard."

A pause.

You have no conditions to make?

Tucker: None.

Lincoln (rising): Mrs. Lincoln and I would wish you to take supper with us.

Tucker: That's very kind, I'm sure. And your answer, Mr. Lincoln?

Lincoln: When you came, you did not know me, Mr. Tucker. You may have something to say now not for my ears.

Tucker: Nothing in the world, I assure—

Lincoln: I will prepare Mrs. Lincoln. You will excuse me for no more than a minute.

He goes out.

Tucker: Well, we might have chosen a handsomer article, but I doubt whether we could have chosen a better.

Hind: He would make a great judge—if you weren't prosecuting.

Price: I'd tell most people, but I'd ask that man.

Tucker: He hasn't given us yes or no yet. Why should he leave us like that, as though plain wasn't plain?

Hind: Perhaps he wanted a thought by himself first.

Macintosh: It wasn't that. But he was right. Abraham Lincoln sees deeper into men's hearts than most. He knows this day will be a memory to us all our lives. Under his eye, which of you could have given play to any untoward thought that had started in you against him since you came into this room? But, leaving you, he knew you could test yourselves to your own ease, and speak the more confident for it, and, if you found yourselves clean of doubt, carry it all the happier in your minds after. Is there a doubt among us?

Tucker:}

Hind:} No, none.

Price:}

Macintosh: Then, Mr. Tucker, ask him again when he comes back.

Tucker: I will.

They sit in silence for a moment, and Lincoln comes in again, back to his place at the table.

Lincoln: I wouldn't have you think it graceless of me to be slow in my answer. But once given, it's for the deep good or the deep ill of all this country. In the face of that a man may well ask himself twenty times, when he's twenty times sure. You make no qualification, any one among you?

Tucker: None. The invitation is as I put it when we sat down. And I would add that we are, all of us, proud to bear it to a man as to whom we feel there is none so fitted to receive it.

Lincoln: I thank you. I accept.

He rises, the others with him. He goes to the door and calls.

Susan.

There is silence. SUSAN comes in.

Susan: Yes, Mr. Lincoln.

Lincoln: Take these gentlemen to Mrs. Lincoln. I will follow at once.

The four men go with SUSAN. LINCOLN stands silently for a moment. He goes again to the map and looks at it. He then turns to the table again, and kneels beside it, possessed and deliberate, burying his face in his hands.

THE CURTAIN FALLS.

The two Chroniclers: Lonely is the man who understands.

Lonely is vision that leads a man away

From the pasture-lands,

From the furrows of corn and the brown loads of hay,

To the mountain-side,

To the high places where contemplation brings

All his adventurings
Among the sowers and the tillers in the wide
Valleys to one fused experience,
That shall control
The courses of his soul,
And give his hand
Courage and continence.
The First Chronicler: Shall a man understand,
He shall know bitterness because his kind,
Being perplexed of mind,
Hold issues even that are nothing mated.
And he shall give
Counsel out of his wisdom that none shall hear;
And steadfast in vain persuasion must he live,
And unabated
Shall his temptation be.
Second Chronicler: Coveting the little, the instant gain,
The brief security,
And easy-tongued renown,
Many will mock the vision that his brain
Builds to a far, unmeasured monument,
And many bid his resolutions down
To the wages of content.
First Chronicler: A year goes by.
The two together: Here contemplate
A heart, undaunted to possess
Itself among the glooms of fate,
In vision and in loneliness.

SCENE II.

Ten months later. Seward's room at Washington. WILLIAM H. SEWARD, Secretary of State, is seated at his table with JOHNSON WHITE and CALEB JENNINGS, representing the Commissioners of the Confederate States.

White: It's the common feeling in the South, Mr. Seward, that you're the one man at Washington to see this thing with large imagination. I say this with no disrespect to the President.

Seward: I appreciate your kindness, Mr. White. But the Union is the Union—you can't get over that. We are faced with a plain fact. Seven of the Southern States have already declared for secession. The President feels—and I may say that I and my colleagues are with him—that to break up the country like that means the decline of America.

Jennings: But everything might be done by compromise, Mr. Seward. Withdraw your garrison from Fort Sumter, Beauregard will be instructed to take no further action, South Carolina will be satisfied with the recognition of her authority, and, as likely as not, be willing to give the lead to the other states in reconsidering secession.

Seward: It is certainly a very attractive and, I conceive, a humane proposal.

White: By furthering it you might be the saviour of the country from civil war, Mr. Seward.

Seward: The President dwelt on his resolution to hold Fort Sumter in his inaugural address. It will be difficult to persuade him to go back on that. He's firm in his decisions.

White: There are people who would call him stubborn. Surely if it were put to him tactfully that so simple a course might avert incalculable disaster, no man would nurse his dignity to the point of not yielding. I speak plainly, but it's a time for plain speaking. Mr. Lincoln is doubtless a man of remarkable qualities: on the two occasions when I have spoken to him I have not been unimpressed. That is so, Mr. Jennings?

Jennings: Certainly.

White: But what does his experience of great affairs of state amount to beside yours, Mr. Seward? He must know how much he depends on certain members of his Cabinet, I might say upon a certain member, for advice.

Seward: We have to move warily.

Jennings: Naturally. A man is sensitive, doubtless, in his first taste of office.

Seward: My support of the President is, of course, unquestionable.

White: Oh, entirely. But how can your support be more valuable than in lending him your unequalled understanding?

Seward: The whole thing is coloured in his mind by the question of slavery.

Jennings: Disabuse his mind. Slavery is nothing. Persuade him to withdraw from Fort Sumter, and slavery can be settled round a table. You know there's a considerable support even for abolition in the South itself. If the trade has to be allowed in some districts, what is that compared to the disaster of civil war?

White: We do not believe that the Southern States wish with any enthusiasm to secede. They merely wish to establish their right to do so. Acknowledge that by evacuating Fort Sumter, and nothing will come of it but a perfectly proper concession to an independence of spirit that is not disloyal to the Union at heart.

Seward: You understand, of course, that I can say nothing officially.

Jennings: These are nothing but informal suggestions.

Seward: But I may tell you that I am not unsympathetic.

White: We were sure that that would be so.

Seward: And my word is not without influence.

Jennings: It can be used to bring you very great credit, Mr. Seward.

Seward: In the mean time, you will say nothing of this interview, beyond making your reports, which should be confidential.

White: You may rely upon us.

Seward (rising with the others): Then I will bid you good-morning.

White: We are profoundly sensible of the magnanimous temper in which we are convinced you will conduct this grave business. Good-morning, Mr. Seward.

Jennings: And I—

There is a knock at the door.

Seward: Yes—come in.

A CLERK comes in.

Clerk: The President is coming up the stairs, sir.

Seward: Thank you.

THE CLERK goes. This is unfortunate. Say nothing, and go at once.

LINCOLN comes in, now whiskered and bearded.

Lincoln: Good-morning, Mr. Seward. Good-morning, gentlemen.

Seward: Good-morning, Mr. President. And I am obliged to you for calling, gentlemen. Good-morning.

He moves towards the door.

Lincoln: Perhaps these gentlemen could spare me ten minutes.

White: It might not—

Lincoln: Say five minutes.

Jennings: Perhaps you would—

Lincoln: I am anxious always for any opportunity to exchange views with our friends of the South. Much enlightenment may be gained in five minutes. Be seated, I beg you—if Mr. Seward will allow us.

Seward: By all means. Shall I leave you?

Lincoln: Leave us—but why? I may want your support, Mr. Secretary, if we should not wholly agree. Be seated, gentlemen.

SEWARD places a chair for LINCOLN, and they sit at the table.

You have messages for us?

White: Well, no, we can't say that.

Lincoln: No messages? Perhaps I am inquisitive?

Seward: These gentlemen are anxious to sound any moderating influences.

Lincoln: I trust they bring moderating influences with them. You will find me a ready listener, gentlemen.

Jennings: It's a delicate matter, Mr. Lincoln. Ours is just an informal visit.

Lincoln: Quite, quite. But we shall lose nothing by knowing each other's minds.

White: Shall we tell the President what we came to say, Mr. Seward?

Lincoln: I shall be grateful. If I should fail to understand, Mr. Seward, no doubt, will enlighten me.

Jennings: We thought it hardly worth while to trouble you at so early a stage.

Lincoln: So early a stage of what?

Jennings: I mean—

Seward: These gentlemen, in a common anxiety for peace, were merely seeking the best channel through which suggestions could be made.

Lincoln: To whom?

Seward: To the government.

Lincoln: The head of the government is here.

White: But—

Lincoln: Come, gentlemen. What is it?

Jennings: It's this matter of Fort Sumter, Mr. President. If you withdraw your garrison from Fort Sumter it won't be looked upon as weakness in you. It will merely be looked upon as a concession to a natural privilege. We believe that the South at heart does not want secession. It wants to establish the right to decide for itself.

Lincoln: The South wants the stamp of national approval upon slavery. It can't have it.

White: Surely that's not the point. There's no law in the South against slavery.

Lincoln: Laws come from opinion, Mr. White. The South knows it.

Jennings: Mr. President, if I may say so, you don't quite understand.

Lincoln: Does Mr. Seward understand?

White: We believe so.

Lincoln: You are wrong. He doesn't understand, because you didn't mean him to. I don't blame you. You think you are acting for the best. You think you've got an honest case. But I'll put your case for you, and I'll put it naked. Many people in this country want abolition; many don't. I'll say nothing for the moment as to the rights and wrongs of it. But every man, whether he wants it or not, knows it may come. Why does the South propose secession? Because it knows abolition may come, and it wants to avoid it. It wants more: it wants the right to extend the slave foundation. We've all been to blame for slavery, but we in the North have been willing to mend our ways. You have not. So you'll secede, and make your own laws. But you weren't prepared for resistance; you don't want resistance. And you hope that if you can tide over the first crisis and make us give way, opinion will prevent us from opposing you with force again, and you'll be able to get your own way about the slave business by threats. That's your case. You didn't say so to Mr. Seward, but it is. Now, I'll give you my answer. Gentlemen, it's no good hiding this thing in a corner. It's got to be settled. I said the other day that Fort Sumter would be held as long as we could hold it. I said it because I know exactly what it means. Why are you investing it? Say, if you like, it's to establish your right of secession with no purpose of exercising it. Why do you want to establish that right? Because now we will allow no extension of slavery, and because some day we may abolish it. You can't deny it; there's no other answer.

Jennings: I see how it is. You may force freedom as much as you like, but we are to beware how we force slavery.

Lincoln: It couldn't be put better, Mr. Jennings. That's what the Union means. It is a Union that stands for common right. That is its foundation—that is why it is for every honest man to preserve it. Be clear about this issue. If there is war, it will not be on the slave question. If the South is loyal to the Union, it can fight slave legislation by constitutional means, and win its way if it can. If it claims the right to secede, then to preserve this country from disruption, to maintain that right to which every state pledged itself when the Union was won for us by our fathers, war may be the only way. We won't break up the Union, and you shan't. In your hands, and not in mine, is the momentous issue of civil war. You can have no conflict without yourselves being the aggressors. I am loath to close. We are not enemies, but friends. We must not be enemies. Though passion may have strained, do not allow it to break our bonds of affection. That is our answer. Tell them that. Will you tell them that?

White: You are determined?

Lincoln: I beg you to tell them.

Jennings: It shall be as you wish.

Lincoln: Implore them to order Beauregard's return. You can telegraph it now, from here. Will you do that?

White: If you wish it.

Lincoln: Earnestly. Mr. Seward, will you please place a clerk at their service. Ask for an answer.

SEWARD rings a bell. A CLERK comes in.

Seward: Give these gentlemen a private wire. Place yourself at their disposal.

Clerk: Yes, sir.

WHITE and JENNINGS go out with the CLERK. For a moment LINCOLN and SEWARD are silent, LINCOLN pacing the room, SEWARD standing at the table.

Lincoln: Seward, this won't do.

Seward: You don't suspect—

Lincoln: I do not. But let us be plain. No man can say how wisely, but Providence has brought me to the leadership of this country, with a task before me greater than that which rested on Washington himself. When I made my Cabinet, you were the first man I chose. I do not regret it. I think I never shall. But remember, faith earns faith. What is it? Why didn't those men come to see me?

Seward: They thought my word might bear more weight with you than theirs.

Lincoln: Your word for what?

Seward: Discretion about Fort Sumter.

Lincoln: Discretion?

Seward: It's devastating, this thought of war.

Lincoln: It is. Do you think I'm less sensible of that than you? War should be impossible. But you can only make it impossible by destroying its causes. Don't you see that to withdraw from Fort Sumter is to do nothing of the kind? If one half of this country claims the right to disown the Union, the claim in the eyes of every true guardian among us must be a cause for war, unless we hold the Union to be a false thing instead of the public consent to decent principles of life that it is. If we withdraw from Fort Sumter, we do nothing to destroy that cause. We can only destroy it by convincing them that secession is a betrayal of their trust. Please God we may do so.

Seward: Has there, perhaps, been some timidity in making all this clear to the country?

Lincoln: Timidity? And you were talking of discretion.

Seward: I mean that perhaps our policy has not been sufficiently defined.

Lincoln: And have you not concurred in all our decisions? Do not deceive yourself. You urge me to discretion in one breath and tax me with timidity in the next. While there was hope that they might call Beauregard back out of their own good sense, I was determined to say nothing to inflame them. Do you call that timidity? Now their intention is clear, and you've heard me speak this morning clearly also. And now you talk about discretion—you, who call what was discretion at the right time, timidity, now counsel timidity at the wrong time, and call it discretion. Seward, you may think I'm simple, but I can see your mind working as plainly as you might see the innards of a clock. You can bring great gifts to this government, with your zeal, and your administrative experience, and your love of men. Don't spoil it by thinking I've got a dull brain.

Seward (slowly): Yes, I see. I've not been thinking quite clearly about it all.

Lincoln (taking a paper from his pocket): Here's the paper you sent me. "Some Thoughts for the President's Consideration. Great Britain ... Russia ... Mexico ... policy. Either the President must control this himself, or devolve it on some member of his Cabinet. It is not in my especial province, but I neither seek to evade nor assume responsibility."

There is a pause, the two men looking at each, other without speaking. LINCOLN hands the paper to SEWARD, who holds it for a moment, tears it up and throws it into his basket.

Seward: I beg your pardon.

Lincoln (taking his hand): That's brave of you.

JOHN HAY, a Secretary, comes in.

Hay: There's a messenger from Major Anderson, sir. He's ridden straight from Fort Sumter.

Lincoln: Take him to my room. No, bring him here.

HAY goes.

Seward: What does it mean?

Lincoln: I don't like the sound of it.

He rings a bell. A CLERK comes in.

Are there any gentlemen of the Cabinet in the house?

Clerk: Mr. Chase and Mr. Blair, I believe, sir.

Lincoln: My compliments to them, and will they be prepared to see me here at once if necessary. Send the same message to any other ministers you can find.

Clerk: Yes, sir.

He goes.

Lincoln: We may have to decide now—now.

HAY shows in a perspiring and dust-covered

MESSENGER, and retires. From Major Anderson?

The Messenger: Yes, sir. Word of mouth, sir.

Lincoln: Your credentials?

The Messenger (giving LINCOLN a paper). Here, sir.

Lincoln (glancing at it): Well?

The Messenger: Major Anderson presents his duty to the government. He can hold the Fort three days more without provisions and reinforcements.

LINCOLN rings the bell, and waits until a third CLERK comes in.

Lincoln: See if Mr. White and Mr. Jennings have had any answer yet. Mr.—what's his name?

Seward: Hawkins.

Lincoln: Mr. Hawkins is attending to them. And ask Mr. Hay to come here.

Clerk: Yes, sir.

He goes. LINCOLN sits at the table and writes. HAY comes in.

Lincoln (writing): Mr. Hay, do you know where General Scott is?

Hay: At headquarters, I think, sir.

Lincoln: Take this to him yourself and bring an answer back.

Hay: Yes, sir.

He takes the note, and goes.

Lincoln: Are things very bad at the Fort?

The Messenger: The major says three days, sir. Most of us would have said twenty-four hours.

A knock at the door.

Seward: Yes.

HAWKINS comes in.

Hawkins: Mr. White is just receiving a message across the wire, sir.

Lincoln: Ask him to come here directly he's finished.

Hawkins: Yes, sir.

He goes. LINCOLN goes to a far door and opens it. He speaks to the MESSENGER.

Lincoln: Will you wait in here?

The MESSENGER goes through.

Seward: Do you mind if I smoke?

Lincoln: Not at all, not at all.

SEWARD lights a cigar.

Three days. If White's message doesn't help us—three days.

Seward: But surely we must withdraw as a matter of military necessity now.

Lincoln: Why doesn't White come?

SEWARD goes to the window and throws it up. He stands looking down into the street. LINCOLN stands at the table looking fixedly at the door. After a moment or two there is a knock.

Come in.

HAWKINS shows in WHITE and JENNINGS, and goes out. SEWARD closes the window.

Well?

White: I'm sorry. They won't give way.

Lincoln: You told them all I said?

Jennings: Everything.

Lincoln: It's critical.

White: They are definite.

LINCOLN paces once or twice up and down the room, standing again at his place at the table.

Lincoln: They leave no opening?

White: I regret to say, none.

Lincoln: It's a grave decision. Terribly grave. Thank you, gentlemen. Good-morning.

White and Jennings: Good-morning, gentlemen.

They go out.

Lincoln: My God! Seward, we need great courage, great faith.

He rings the bell. The SECOND CLERK comes in.

Did you take my messages?

The Clerk: Yes, sir. Mr. Chase and Mr. Blair are here. The other ministers are coming immediately.

Lincoln: Ask them to come here at once. And send Mr. Hay in directly he returns.

The Clerk: Yes, sir.

He goes.

Lincoln (after a pause): "There is a tide in the affairs of men ..." Do you read Shakespeare, Seward?

Seward: Shakespeare? No.

Lincoln: Ah!

SALMON P. CHASE, Secretary of the Treasury, and MONTGOMERY BLAIR, Postmaster-General, come in.

Good-morning, Mr. Chase, Mr. Blair.

Seward: Good-morning, gentlemen.

Blair: Good-morning, Mr. President. How d'ye do, Mr. Seward.

Chase: Good-morning, Mr. President. Something urgent?

Lincoln: Let us be seated.

As they draw chairs up to the table, the other members of the Cabinet, SIMON CAMERON, CALEB SMITH, BURNET HOOK, and GIDEON WELLES, come in. There is an exchange of greetings, while they arrange themselves round the table.

Gentlemen, we meet in a crisis, the most fateful, perhaps, that has ever faced any government in this country. It can be stated briefly. A message has just come from Anderson. He can hold Fort Sumter three days at most unless we send men and provisions.

Cameron: How many men?

Lincoln: I shall know from Scott in a few minutes how many are necessary.

Welles: Suppose we haven't as many.

Lincoln: Then it's a question of provisioning. We may not be able to do enough to be effective. The question is whether we shall do as much as we can.

Hook: If we withdrew altogether, wouldn't it give the South a lead towards compromise, as being an acknowledgment of their authority, while leaving us free to plead military necessity if we found public opinion dangerous?

Lincoln: My mind is clear. To do less than we can do, whatever that may be, will be fundamentally to allow the South's claim to right of secession. That is my opinion. If you evade the question now, you will have to answer it tomorrow.

Blair: I agree with the President.

Hook: We ought to defer action as long as possible. I consider that we should withdraw.

Lincoln: Don't you see that to withdraw may postpone war, but that it will make it inevitable in the end?

Smith: It is inevitable if we resist.

Lincoln: I fear it will be so. But in that case we shall enter it with uncompromised principles. Mr. Chase?

Chase: It is difficult. But, on the whole, my opinion is with yours, Mr. President.

Lincoln: And you, Seward?

Seward: I respect your opinion, but I must differ.

A knock at the door.

Lincoln: Come in.

HAY comes in. He gives a letter to LINCOLN and goes.

(Reading): Scott says twenty thousand men.

Seward: We haven't ten thousand ready.

Lincoln: It remains a question of sending provisions. I charge you, all of you, to weigh this thing with all your understanding. To temporise now, cannot, in my opinion, avert war. To speak plainly to the world in standing by our resolution to hold Fort Sumter with all our means, and in a plain declaration that the Union must be preserved, will leave us with a clean cause, simply and loyally supported. I tremble at the thought of war. But we have in our hands a sacred trust. It is threatened. We have had no thought of aggression. We have been the aggressed. Persuasion has failed, and I conceive it to be our duty to resist. To withhold supplies from Anderson would be to deny that duty. Gentlemen, the matter is before you.

A pause.

For provisioning the fort?

LINCOLN, CHASE, and BLAIR hold up their hands.

For immediate withdrawal?

SEWARD, CAMERON, SMITH, HOOK, and WELLES hold up their hands. There is a pause of some moments.

Gentlemen, I may have to take upon myself the responsibility of over-riding your vote. It will be for me to satisfy Congress and public opinion. Should I receive any resignations?

There is silence.

I thank you for your consideration, gentlemen. That is all.

They rise, and the Ministers, with the exception of SEWARD, go out, talking as they pass beyond the door.

You are wrong, Seward, wrong.

Seward: I believe you. I respect your judgment even as far as that. But I must speak as I feel.

Lincoln: May I speak to this man alone?

Seward: Certainly. He goes out. LINCOLN stands motionless for a moment. Then he moves to a map of the United States, much larger than the one in his Illinois home, and looks at it as he did there. He goes to the far door and opens it.

Lincoln: Will you come in?

The MESSENGER comes.

Can you ride back to Major Anderson at once?

The Messenger: Yes, sir.

Lincoln: Tell him that we cannot reinforce him immediately. We haven't the men.

The Messenger: Yes, sir.

Lincoln: And say that the first convoy of supplies will leave Washington this evening.

The Messenger: Yes, sir.

Lincoln: Thank you.

The MESSENGER goes. LINCOLN stands at the table for a moment; he rings the bell. HAWKINS comes in.

Mr. Hay, please.

Hawkins: Yes, sir.

He goes, and a moment later HAY comes in.

Lincoln: Go to General Scott. Ask him to come to me at once.

Hay: Yes, sir.

He goes.

THE CURTAIN FALLS.

The two Chroniclers: You who have gone gathering
 Cornflowers and meadowsweet,
Heard the hazels glancing down
 On September eves,
Seen the homeward rooks on wing
 Over fields of golden wheat,
And the silver cups that crown
 Water-lily leaves;
You who know the tenderness
 Of old men at eve-tide,
Coming from the hedgerows,
 Coming from the plough,
And the wandering caress
 Of winds upon the woodside,
When the crying yaffle goes
 Underneath the bough;
First Chronicler: You who mark the flowing

Of sap upon the May-time,
And the waters welling
From the watershed,
You who count the growing
Of harvest and hay-time,
Knowing these the telling
Of your daily bread;
Second Chronicler: You who cherish courtesy
With your fellows at your gate,
And about your hearthstone sit
Under love's decrees,
You who know that death will be
Speaking with you soon or late,
The two together: Kinsmen, what is
mother-wit
But the light of these?
Knowing these, what is there more
For learning in your little years?
Are not these all gospels bright
Shining on your day?
How then shall your hearts be sore
With envy and her brood of fears,
How forget the words of light
From the mountain-way? ...
Blessed are the merciful....
Does not every threshold seek
Meadows and the flight of birds
For compassion still?
Blessed are the merciful....
Are we pilgrims yet to speak

Out of Olivet the words
Of knowledge and good-will?
First Chronicler: Two years of darkness, and this man but grows
Greater in resolution, more constant in compassion.
He goes
The way of dominion in pitiful, high-hearted fashion.

SCENE III.

Nearly two years later.

A small reception room at the White House. MRS. LINCOLN, dressed in a fashion perhaps a little too considered, despairing as she now does of any sartorial grace in her husband, and acutely conscious that she must meet this necessity of office alone, is writing. She rings the bell, and SUSAN, who has taken her promotion more philosophically, comes in.

Mrs. Lincoln: Admit any one who calls, Susan. And enquire whether the President will be in to tea.

Susan: Mr. Lincoln has just sent word that he will be in.

Mrs. Lincoln: Very well.

SUSAN is going.

Susan. Susan: Yes, ma'am.

Mrs. Lincoln: You still say Mr. Lincoln. You should say the President.

Susan: Yes, ma'am. But you see, ma'am, it's difficult after calling him Mr. Lincoln for fifteen years.

Mrs. Lincoln: But you must remember. Everybody calls him the President now.

Susan: No, ma'am. There's a good many people call him Father Abraham now. And there's some that like him even better than that. Only to-day Mr. Coldpenny, at the stores, said, "Well, Susan, and how 's old Abe this morning?"

Mrs. Lincoln: I hope you don't encourage them.

Susan: Oh, no, ma'am. I always refer to him as Mr. Lincoln.

Mrs. Lincoln: Yes, but you must say the President.

Susan: I'm afraid I shan't ever learn, ma'am.

Mrs. Lincoln: You must try.

Susan: Yes, of course, ma'am.

Mrs. Lincoln: And bring any visitors up.

Susan: Yes, ma'am. There's a lady waiting now.

Mrs. Lincoln: Then why didn't you say so?

Susan: That's what I was going to, ma'am, when you began to talk about Mr.—I mean the President, ma'am.

Mrs. Lincoln: Well, show her up.

SUSAN goes. MRS. LINCOLN closes her writing desk. SUSAN returns, showing in MRS. GOLIATH BLOW.

Susan: Mrs. Goliath Blow.

She goes.

Mrs. Blow: Good-afternoon, Mrs. Lincoln.

Mrs. Lincoln: Good-afternoon, Mrs. Blow. Sit down, please.

They sit.

Mrs. Blow: And is the dear President well?

Mrs. Lincoln: Yes. He's rather tired.

Mrs. Blow: Of course, to be sure. This dreadful war. But I hope he's not getting tired of the war.

Mrs. Lincoln: It's a constant anxiety for him. He feels his responsibility very deeply.

Mrs. Blow: To be sure. But you mustn't let him get war-weary. These monsters in the South have got to be stamped out.

Mrs. Lincoln: I don't think you need be afraid of the President's firmness.

Mrs. Blow: Oh, of course not. I was only saying to Goliath yesterday, "The President will never give way till he has the South squealing," and Goliath agreed.

SUSAN comes in.

Susan: Mrs. Otherly, ma'am.

Mrs. Lincoln: Show Mrs. Otherly in.

SUSAN goes

Mrs. Blow: Oh, that dreadful woman! I believe she wants the war to stop.

Susan (at the door): Mrs. Otherly.

MRS. OTHERLY comes in and SUSAN goes.

Mrs. Lincoln: Good-afternoon, Mrs. Otherly. You know Mrs. Goliath Blow?

Mrs. Otherly: Yes. Good-afternoon. She sits.

Mrs. Blow: Goliath says the war will go on for another three years at least.

Mrs. Otherly: Three years? That would be terrible, wouldn't it?

Mrs. Blow: We must be prepared to make sacrifices.

Mrs. Otherly: Yes.

Mrs. Blow: It makes my blood boil to think of those people.

Mrs. Otherly: I used to know a lot of them. Some of them were very kind and nice.

Mrs. Blow: That was just their cunning, depend on it. I'm afraid there's a good deal of disloyalty among us. Shall we see the dear President this afternoon, Mrs. Lincoln?

Mrs. Lincoln: He will be here directly, I think.

Mrs. Blow: You 're looking wonderfully well, with all the hard work that you have to do. I've really had to drop some of mine. And with expenses going up, it's all very lowering, don't you think? Goliath and I have had to reduce several of our subscriptions. But, of course, we all have to deny ourselves something. Ah, good-afternoon, dear Mr. President.

LINCOLN comes in. THE LADIES rise and shake hands with him.

Lincoln: Good-afternoon, ladies.

Mrs. Otherly: Good-afternoon, Mr. President.

They all sit.

Mrs. Blow: And is there any startling news, Mr. President?

Lincoln: Madam, every morning when I wake up, and say to myself, a hundred, or two hundred, or a thousand of my countrymen will be killed to-day, I find it startling.

Mrs. Blow: Oh, yes, of course, to be sure. But I mean, is there any good news.

Lincoln: Yes. There is news of a victory. They lost twenty-seven hundred men—we lost eight hundred.

Mrs. Blow: How splendid!

Lincoln: Thirty-five hundred.

Mrs. Blow: Oh, but you mustn't talk like that, Mr. President. There were only eight hundred that mattered.

Lincoln: The world is larger than your heart, madam.

Mrs. Blow: Now the dear President is becoming whimsical, Mrs. Lincoln.

SUSAN brings in tea-tray, and hands tea round. LINCOLN takes none. SUSAN goes.

Mrs. Otherly: Mr. President.

Lincoln: Yes, ma'am.

Mrs. Otherly: I don't like to impose upon your hospitality. I know how difficult everything is for you. But one has to take one's opportunities. May I ask you a question?

Lincoln: Certainly, ma'am.

Mrs. Otherly: Isn't it possible for you to stop this war? In the name of a suffering country, I ask you that.

Mrs. Blow: I'm sure such a question would never have entered my head.

Lincoln: It is a perfectly right question. Ma'am, I have but one thought always—how can this thing be stopped? But we must ensure the integrity of the Union. In two years war has become an hourly bitterness to me. I believe I suffer no less than any man. But it must be endured. The cause was a right one two years ago. It is unchanged.

Mrs. Otherly: I know you are noble and generous. But I believe that war must be wrong under any circumstances, for any cause.

Mrs. Blow: I'm afraid the President would have but little encouragement if he listened often to this kind of talk.

Lincoln: I beg you not to harass yourself, madam. Ma'am, I too believe war to be wrong. It is the weakness and the jealousy and the folly of men that make a thing so wrong possible. But we are all weak, and jealous, and foolish. That's how the world is, ma'am, and we cannot outstrip the world. Some of the worst of us are sullen, aggressive still—just clumsy, greedy pirates. Some of us have grown out of that. But the best of us have an instinct to resist aggression if it won't listen to persuasion. You may say it's a wrong instinct. I don't know. But it's there, and it's there in millions of good men. I don't believe it's a wrong instinct, I believe that the world must come to wisdom slowly. It is for us who hate aggression to persuade men always and earnestly against it, and hope that, little by little, they will hear us. But in the mean time there will come moments when the aggressors will force the instinct to resistance to act. Then we must act earnestly, praying always in our courage that never again will this thing happen. And then we must turn again, and again, and again to persuasion. This appeal to force is the misdeed of an imperfect world. But we are imperfect. We must strive to purify the world, but we must not think ourselves pure above the world. When I had this thing to decide, it would have been easy to say, "No, I will have none of it; it is evil, and I will not touch it." But that would have decided nothing, and I saw what I believed to be the truth as I now put it to you, ma'am. It's a forlorn thing for any man to have this responsibility in his heart. I may see wrongly, but that's how I see.

Mrs. Blow: I quite agree with you, Mr. President. These brutes in the South must be taught, though I doubt whether you can teach them anything except by destroying them. That's what Goliath says.

Lincoln: Goliath must be getting quite an old man.

Mrs. Blow: Indeed, he's not, Mr. President Goliath is only thirty-eight.

Lincoln: Really, now? Perhaps I might be able to get him a commission.

Mrs. Blow: Oh, no. Goliath couldn't be spared. He's doing contracts for the government, you know. Goliath couldn't possibly go.

I'm sure he will be very pleased when I tell him what you say about these people who want to stop the war, Mr. President. I hope Mrs. Otherly is satisfied. Of course, we could all complain. We all have to make sacrifices, as I told Mrs. Otherly.

Mrs. Otherly: Thank you, Mr. President, for what you've said. I must try to think about it. But I always believed war to be wrong. I didn't want my boy to go, because I believed it to be wrong. But he would. That came to me last week.

She hands a paper to LINCOLN.

Lincoln (looks at it, rises, and hands it back to her): Ma'am, there are times when no man may speak. I grieve for you, I grieve for you.

Mrs. Otherly (rising): I think I will go. You don't mind my saying what I did?

Lincoln: We are ail poor creatures, ma'am. Think kindly of me. (He takes her hand.) Mary.

MRS. LINCOLN goes out with MRS. OTHERLY.

Mrs. Blow: Of course it's very sad for her, poor woman. But she makes her trouble worse by these perverted views, doesn't she? And, I hope you will show no signs of weakening, Mr. President, till it has been made impossible for those shameful rebels to hold up their heads again. Goliath says you ought to make a proclamation that no mercy will be shown to them afterwards. I'm sure I shall never speak to one of them again.

Rising.

Well, I must be going. I'll see Mrs. Lincoln as I go out. Good-afternoon, Mr. President. She turns at the door, and offers LINCOLN her handy which he does not take.

Lincoln: Good-afternoon, madam. And I'd like to offer ye a word of advice. That poor mother told me what she thought. I don't agree with her, but I honour her. She's wrong, but she is noble. You've told me what you think. I don't agree with you, and I'm ashamed of you and your like. You, who have sacrificed nothing, babble about destroying the South while other people conquer it. I accepted this war with a sick heart, and I've a heart that's near to breaking every day. I accepted it in the name of humanity, and just and merciful dealing, and the hope of love and charity on earth. And you come to me, talking of revenge and destruction, and malice, and enduring hate. These gentle people are mistaken, but they are mistaken cleanly, and in a great name. It is you that dishonour the cause for which we stand—it is you who would make it a mean and little thing. Good-afternoon.

He opens the door and MRS. BLOW, finding words inadequate, goes. LINCOLN moves across the room and rings a bell. After a moment, SUSAN comes in. Susan, if that lady comes here again she may meet with an accident.

Susan: Yes, sir. Is that all, sir?

Lincoln: No, sir, it is not all, sir. I don't like this coat. I am going to change it. I shall be back in a minute or two, and if a gentleman named Mr. William Custis calls, ask him to wait in here.

He goes out. SUSAN collects the teacups. As she is going to the door a quiet, grave white-haired negro appears facing her. SUSAN starts violently.

The Negro (he talks slowly and very quietly): It is all right.

Susan: And who in the name of night might you be?

The Negro: Mista William Custis. Mista Lincoln tell me to come here. Nobody stop me, so I come to look for him.

Susan: Are you Mr. William Custis?

Custis: Yes.

Susan: Mr. Lincoln will be here directly. He's gone to change his coat. You'd better sit down.

Custis: Yes.

He does so, looking about him with a certain pathetic inquisitiveness. Mista Lincoln live here. You his servant? A very fine thing for young girl to be servant to Mista Lincoln.

Susan: Well, we get on very well together.

Custis: A very bad thing to be slave in South.

Susan: Look here, you Mr. Custis, don't you go mixing me up with slaves.

Custis: No, you not slave. You servant, but you free body. That very mighty thing. A poor servant, born free.

Susan: Yes, but look here, are you pitying me, with your poor servant?

Custis: Pity? No. I think you very mighty.

Susan: Well, I don't know so much about mighty. But I expect you're right. It isn't every one that rises to the White House.

Custis: It not every one that is free body. That is why you mighty.

Susan: I've never thought much about it.

Custis: I think always about it.

Susan: I suppose you're free, aren't you?

Custis: Yes. Not born free. I was beaten when I a little nigger. I saw my mother—I will not remember what I saw.

Susan: I'm sorry, Mr. Custis. That was wrong.

Custis: Yes. Wrong.

Susan: Are all nig—I mean are all black gentlemen like you?

Custis: No. I have advantages. They not many have advantages.

Susan: No, I suppose not. Here's Mr. Lincoln coming.

LINCOLN, coated after his heart's desire, comes to the door. CUSTIS rises. This is the gentleman you said, sir.

She goes out with the tray.

Lincoln: Mr. Custis, I'm very glad to see you. He offers his hand. CUSTIS takes it, and is about to kiss it. LINCOLN stops him gently. (Sitting): Sit down, will you? Custis (still standing, keeping his hat in his hand): It very kind of Mista Lincoln ask me to come to see him.

Lincoln: I was afraid you might refuse.

Custis: A little shy? Yes. But so much to ask Glad to come.

Lincoln: Please sit down.

Custis: Polite?

Lincoln: Please. I can't sit myself, you see, if you don't.

Custis: Black, black. White, white.

Lincoln: Nonsense. Just two old men, sitting together (CUSTIS sits to LINCOLN'S gesture)—and talking.

Custis: I think I older man than Mista Lincoln.

Lincoln: Yes, I expect you are, I'm fifty-four.

Custis: I seventy-two.

Lincoln: I hope I shall look as young when I'm seventy-two.

Custis: Cold water. Much walk. Believe in Lord Jesus Christ. Have always little herbs learnt when a little nigger. Mista Lincoln try. Very good.

He hands a small twist of paper to LINCOLN.

Lincoln: Now, that's uncommon kind of you. Thank you. I've heard much about your preaching, Mr. Custis.

Custis: Yes.

Lincoln: I should like to hear you.

Custis: Mista Lincoln great friend of my people.

Lincoln: I have come at length to a decision.

Custis: A decision?

Lincoln: Slavery is going. We have been resolved always to confine it. Now it shall be abolished.

Custis: You sure?

Lincoln: Sure.

CUSTIS slowly stands up, bows his head, and sits again.

Custis: My people much to learn. Years, and years, and years. Ignorant, frightened, suspicious people. It will be difficult, very slow. (With growing passion.) But born free bodies. Free. I born slave, Mista Lincoln. No man understand who not born slave.

Lincoln: Yes, yes. I understand.

Custis (with his normal regularity): I think so. Yes.

Lincoln: I should like you to ask me any question you wish.

Custis: I have some complaint. Perhaps I not understand.

Lincoln: Tell me.

Custis: Southern soldiers take some black men prisoner. Black men in your uniform. Take them prisoner. Then murder them.

Lincoln: I know.

Custis: What you do?

Lincoln: We have sent a protest.

Custis: No good. Must do more.

Lincoln: What more can we do?

Custis: You know.

Lincoln: Yes; but don't ask me for reprisals.

Custis (gleaming): Eye for an eye, tooth for a tooth.

Lincoln: No, no. You must think. Think what you are saying.

Custis: I think of murdered black men.

Lincoln: You would not ask me to murder?

Custis: Punish—not murder.

Lincoln: Yes, murder. How can I kill men in cold blood for what has been done by others? Think what would follow. It is for us to set a great example, not to follow a wicked one. You do believe that, don't you?

Custis (after a pause): I know. Yes. Let your light so shine before men. I trust Mista Lincoln. Will trust. I was wrong. I was too sorry for my people.

Lincoln: Will you remember this? For more than two years I have thought of you every day. I have grown a weary man with thinking. But I shall not forget. I promise that.

Custis: You great, kind friend. I will love you.

A knock at the door.

Lincoln: Yes.

SUSAN comes in.

Susan: An officer gentleman. He says it's very important.

Lincoln: I'll come.

He and CUSTIS rise.

Wait, will you, Mr. Custis? I want to ask you some questions.

He goes out. It is getting dark, and SUSAN lights a lamp and draws the curtains. CUSTIS stands by the door looking after LINCOLN.

Custis: He very good man.

Susan: You've found that out, have you?

Custis: Do you love him, you white girl?

Susan: Of course I do.

Custis: Yes, you must.

Susan: He's a real white man. No offence, of course.

Custis: Not offend. He talk to me as if black no difference.

Susan: But I tell you what, Mr. Custis. He'll kill himself over this war, his heart's that kind—like a shorn lamb, as they say.

Custis: Very unhappy war.

Susan: But I suppose he's right. It's got to go on till it's settled.

In the street below a body of people is heard approaching, singing "John Brown's Body" CUSTIS and SUSAN stand listening, SUSAN joining in the song as it passes and fades away.

THE CURTAIN FALLS.

First Chronicler: Unchanged our time. And further yet

In loneliness must be the way,

And difficult and deep the debt

Of constancy to pay.

Second Chronicler: And one denies,

and one forsakes.

And still unquestioning he goes,

Who has his lonely thoughts, and makes.

A world of those.

The two together: When the high heart we magnify,

And the sure vision celebrate,

And worship greatness passing by,

Ourselves are great.

SCENE IV.

About the same date. A meeting of the Cabinet at Washington. SMITH has gone and CAMERON has been replaced by EDWIN M. STANTON, Secretary of War. Otherwise the ministry, completed by SEWARD, CHASE, HOOK, BLAIR, and WELLES, is as before. They are now arranging themselves at the table, leaving LINCOLN'S place empty.

Seward (coming in): I've just had my summons. Is there some special news?

Stanton: Yes. McClellan has defeated Lee at Antietam. It's our greatest success. They ought not to recover from it. The tide is turning.

Blair: Have you seen the President?

Stanton: I've just been with him.

Welles: What does he say?

Stanton: He only said, "At last." He's coming directly.

Hook: He will bring up his proclamation again. In my opinion it is inopportune.

Seward: Well, we've learnt by now that the President is the best man among us.

Hook: There's a good deal of feeling against him everywhere, I find.

Blair: He's the one man with character enough for this business.

Hook: There are other opinions.

Seward: Yes, but not here, surely.

Hook: It's not for me to say. But I ask you, what does he mean about emancipation? I've always understood that it was the Union we were fighting for, and that abolition was to be kept in our minds for legislation at the right moment. And now one day he talks as though emancipation were his only concern, and the next as though he would throw up the whole idea, if by doing it he could secure peace with the establishment of the Union. Where are we?

Seward: No, you're wrong. It's the Union first now with him, but there's no question about his views on slavery. You know that perfectly well. But he has always kept his policy about slavery free in his mind, to be directed as he thought best for the sake of the Union. You remember his words: "If I could save the Union without freeing any slaves, I would do it; and if I could save it by freeing all the slaves, I would do it; and if I could save it by freeing some and leaving others alone, I would also do that. My paramount object in this struggle is to save the Union." Nothing could be plainer than that, just as nothing could be plainer than his determination to free the slaves when he can.

Hook: Well, there are some who would have acted differently.

Blair: And you may depend upon it they would not have acted so wisely.

Stanton: I don't altogether agree with the President. But he's the only man I should agree with at all.

Hook: To issue the proclamation now, and that's what he will propose, mark my words, will be to confuse the public mind just when we want to keep it clear.

Welles: Are you sure he will propose to issue it now?

Hook: You see if he doesn't.

Welles: If he does I shall support him.

Seward: Is Lee's army broken?

Stanton: Not yet—but it is in grave danger.

Hook: Why doesn't the President come? One would think this news was nothing.

Chase: I must say I'm anxious to know what he has to say about it all.

A CLERK comes in.

Clerk: The President's compliments, and he will be here in a moment.

He goes.

Hook: I shall oppose it if it comes up.

Chase: He may say nothing about it.

Seward: I think he will.

Stanton: Anyhow, it's the critical moment.

Blair: Here he comes.

LINCOLN comes in carrying a small book.

Lincoln: Good-morning, gentlemen.

He takes his place.

The Ministers: Good-morning, Mr. President.

Seward: Great news, we hear.

Hook: If we leave things with the army to take their course for a little now, we ought to see through our difficulties.

Lincoln: It's an exciting morning, gentlemen. I feel rather excited myself. I find my mind not at its best in excitement. Will you allow me?

Opening his book.

It may compose us all. It is Mr. Artemus Ward's latest.

THE MINISTERS, with the exception of HOOK, who makes no attempt to hide his irritation, and STANTON, who would do the same but for his disapproval of HOOK, listen with good-humoured patience and amusement while he reads the following passage from Artemus Ward.

"High Handed Outrage at Utica."

"In the Faul of 1856, I showed my show in Utiky, a trooly grate city in the State of New York. The people gave me a cordyal recepshun. The press was loud in her prases. 1 day as I was givin a descripshun of my Beests and Snaiks in my usual flowry stile what was my skorn and disgust to see a big burly feller walk up to the cage containin my wax figgers of the Lord's last Supper, and cease Judas Iscarrot by the feet and drag him out on the ground. He then commenced fur to pound him as hard as he cood."

"'What under the son are you abowt,' cried I."

"Sez he, 'What did you bring this pussylanermus cuss here fur?' and he hit the wax figger another tremenjis blow on the bed."

"Sez I, 'You egrejus ass, that airs a wax figger—a representashun of the false 'Postle.'"

"Sez he, 'That's all very well fur you to say; but I tell you, old man, that Judas Iscarrot can't show himself in Utiky with impunerty by a darn site,' with which observashun he kaved in Judassis hed. The young man belonged to 1 of the first famerlies in Utiky. I sood him, and the Joory brawt in a verdick of Arson in the 3d degree."

Stanton: May we now consider affairs of state?

Hook: Yes, we may.

Lincoln: Mr. Hook says, yes, we may.

Stanton: Thank you.

Lincoln: Oh, no. Thank Mr. Hook.

Seward: McClellan is in pursuit of Lee, I suppose.

Lincoln: You suppose a good deal. But for the first time McClellan has the chance of being in pursuit of Lee, and that's the first sign of their end. If McClellan doesn't take his chance, we'll move Grant down to the job. That will mean delay, but no matter. The mastery has changed hands.

Blair: Grant drinks.

Lincoln: Then tell me the name of his brand. I'll send some barrels to the others. He wins victories.

Hook: Is there other business?

Lincoln: There is. Some weeks ago I showed you a draft I made proclaiming freedom for all slaves.

Hook (aside to Welles): I told you so.

Lincoln: You thought then it was not the time to issue it. I agreed. I think the moment has come. May I read it to you again? "It is proclaimed that on the first day of January in the year of our Lord one thousand eight hundred and sixty-three, all persons held as slaves within any state, the people whereof shall then be in rebellion against the United States, shall be then, thenceforward, and forever free."

That allows three months from to-day. There are clauses dealing with compensation in a separate draft.

Hook: I must oppose the issue of such a proclamation at this moment in the most unqualified terms. This question should be left until our victory is complete. To thrust it forward now would be to invite dissension when we most need unity.

Welles: I do not quite understand, Mr. President, why you think this the precise moment.

Lincoln: Believe me, gentlemen, I have considered this matter with all the earnestness and understanding of which I am capable.

Hook: But when the "New York Tribune" urged you to come forward with a clear declaration six months ago, you rebuked them.

Lincoln: Because I thought the occasion not the right one. It was useless to issue a proclamation that might be as inoperative as the Pope's bull against the comet. My duty, it has seemed to me, has been to be loyal to a principle, and not to betray it by expressing it in action at the wrong time. That is what I conceive statesmanship to be. For long now I have had two fixed resolves. To preserve the Union, and to abolish slavery. How to preserve the Union I was always clear, and more than two years of bitterness have not dulled my vision. We have fought for the Union, and we are now winning for the Union. When and how to proclaim abolition I have all this time been uncertain. I am uncertain no longer. A few weeks ago I saw that, too, clearly. So soon, I said to myself, as the rebel army shall be driven out of Maryland, and it becomes plain to the world that victory is assured to us in the end, the time will have come to announce that with that victory and a vindicated Union will come abolition. I made the promise to myself—and to my Maker. The rebel army is now driven out, and I am going to fulfil that promise. I do not wish your advice about the main matter, for that I have determined for myself. This I say without intending anything but respect for any one of you. But I beg you to stand with me in this thing.

Hook: In my opinion, it's altogether too impetuous.

Lincoln: One other observation I will make. I know very well that others might in this matter, as in others, do better than I can, and if

I was satisfied that the public confidence was more fully possessed by any one of them than by me, and knew of any constitutional way in which he could be put in my place, he should have it. I would gladly yield it to him. But, though I cannot claim undivided confidence, I do not know that, all things considered, any other person has more; and, however this may be, there is no way in which I can have any other man put where I am. I am here; I must do the best I can, and bear the responsibility of taking the course which I feel I ought to take.

Stanton: Could this be left over a short time for consideration?

Chase: I feel that we should remember that our only public cause at the moment is the preservation of the Union.

Hook: I entirely agree.

Lincoln: Gentlemen, we cannot escape history. We of this administration will be remembered in spite of ourselves. No personal significance or insignificance can spare one or another of us. In giving freedom to the slave we assure freedom to the free. We shall nobly save or meanly lose the last, best hope on earth.

He places the proclamation in front of him.

"Shall be thenceforward and forever free."

Gentlemen, I pray for your support.

He signs it.

THE MINISTERS rise. SEWARD, WELLES, and BLAIR shake LINCOLN'S hand and go out. STANTON and CHASE bow to him, and follow. HOOK, the last to rise, moves away, making no sign.

Lincoln: Hook.

Hook: Yes, Mr. President.

Lincoln: Hook, one cannot help hearing things.

Hook: I beg your pardon?

Lincoln: Hook, there's a way some people have, when a man says a disagreeable thing, of asking him to repeat it, hoping to embarrass him. It's often effective. But I'm not easily embarrassed. I said one cannot help hearing things.

Hook: And I do not understand what you mean, Mr. President.

Lincoln: Come, Hook, we're alone. Lincoln is a good enough name. And I think you understand.

Hook: How should I?

Lincoln: Then, plainly, there are intrigues going on.

Hook: Against the government?

Lincoln: No. In it. Against me.

Hook: Criticism, perhaps.

Lincoln: To what end? To better my ways?

Hook: I presume that might be the purpose.

Lincoln: Then, why am I not told what it is?

Hook: I imagine it's a natural compunction.

Lincoln: Or ambition?

Hook: What do you mean?

Lincoln: You think you ought to be in my place.

Hook: You are well informed.

Lincoln: You cannot imagine why every one does not see that you ought to be in my place.

Hook: By what right do you say that?

Lincoln: Is it not true?

Hook: You take me unprepared. You have me at a disadvantage.

Lincoln: You speak as a very scrupulous man, Hook.

Hook: Do you question my honour?

Lincoln: As you will.

Hook: Then I resign.

Lincoln: As a protest against ...?

Hook: Your suspicion.

Lincoln: It is false?

Hook: Very well, I will be frank. I mistrust your judgment.

Lincoln: In what?

Hook: Generally. You over-emphasise abolition.

Lincoln: You don't mean that. You mean that you fear possible public feeling against abolition.

Hook: It must be persuaded, not forced.

Lincoln: All the most worthy elements in it are persuaded. But the ungenerous elements make the most noise, and you hear them only. You will run from the terrible name of Abolitionist even when it is pronounced by worthless creatures whom you know you have every reason to despise.

Hook: You have, in my opinion, failed in necessary firmness in saying what will be the individual penalties of rebellion.

Lincoln: This is a war. I will not allow it to become a blood-feud.

Hook: We are fighting treason. We must meet it with severity.

Lincoln: We will defeat treason. And I will meet it with conciliation.

Hook: It is a policy of weakness.

Lincoln: It is a policy of faith—it is a policy of compassion. (Warmly.) Hook, why do you plague me with these jealousies? Once before I found a member of my Cabinet working behind my back. But he was disinterested, and he made amends nobly. But, Hook, you have allowed the burden of these days to sour you. I know it all. I've watched you plotting and plotting for authority. And I, who am a lonely man, have been sick at heart. So great is the task God has given to my hand, and so few are my days, and my deepest hunger is always for loyalty in my own house. You have withheld it from me. You have done great service in your office, but you have grown envious. Now you resign, as you did once before when I came openly to you in friendship. And you think that again I shall flatter you and coax you to stay. I don't think I ought to do it. I will not do it. I must take you at your word.

Hook: I am content.

He turns to go.

Lincoln: Will you shake hands?

Hook: I beg you will excuse me.

He goes. LINCOLN stands silently for a moment, a travelled, lonely captain. He rings a bell, and a CLERK comes in.

Lincoln: Ask Mr. Hay to come in.

Clerk: Yes, sir.

He goes. LINCOLN, from the folds of his pockets, produces another book, and holds it unopened. HAY comes in.

Lincoln: I'm rather tired to-day, Hay. Read to me a little. (He hands him the book.) "The Tempest"—you know the passage.

Hay (reading):

Our revels now are ended; these our actors,
As I foretold you, were all spirits, and
Are melted into air, into thin air;
And, like the baseless fabric of this vision,
The cloud-capp'd towers, the gorgeous palaces,
The solemn temples, the great globe itself,
Yea, all which it inherit, shall dissolve
And, like this insubstantial pageant faded,
Leave not a rack behind. We are such stuff
As dreams are made on, and our little life
Is rounded with a sleep.

Lincoln: We are such stuff As dreams are made on, and our little life ...

THE CURTAIN FALLS.

First Chronicler: Two years again.
Desolation of battle, and long debate,
Counsels and prayers of men,
And bitterness of destruction and witless hate,
And the shame of lie contending with lie,
Are spending themselves, and the brain
That set its lonely chart four years gone by,
Knowing the word fulfilled,
Comes with charity and communion to bring

To reckoning,
To reconcile and build.
The two together: What victor coming from the field
  Leaving the victim desolate,
But has a vulnerable shield
  Against the substances of fate?
That battle's won that leads in chains
  But retribution and despite,
And bids misfortune count her gains
  Not stricken in a penal night.
His triumph is but bitterness
  Who looks not to the starry doom
When proud and humble but possess
  The little kingdom of the tomb.
Who, striking home, shall not forgive,
  Strikes with a weak returning rod,
Claiming a fond prerogative
  Against the armoury of God.
Who knows, and for his knowledge stands
  Against the darkness in dispute,
And dedicates industrious hands,
  And keeps a spirit resolute,
Prevailing in the battle, then
  A steward of his word is made,
To bring it honour among men,
  Or know his captaincy betrayed.

SCENE V.

An April evening in 1865. A farmhouse near Appomattox. GENERAL GRANT, Commander-in-Chief, under Lincoln, of the Northern armies, is seated at a table with CAPTAIN MALINS, an aide-de-camp. He is smoking a cigar, and at intervals he replenishes his glass of whiskey. DENNIS, an orderly, sits at a table in the corner, writing.

Grant (consulting a large watch lying in front of him): An hour and a half. There ought to be something more from Meade by now. Dennis.

Dennis (coming to the table): Yes, sir.

Grant: Take these papers to Captain Templeman, and ask Colonel West if the twenty-third are in action yet. Tell the cook to send some soup at ten o'clock. Say it was cold yesterday.

Dennis: Yes, sir.

He goes.

Grant: Give me that map, Malins.

MALINS hands him the map at which he is working.

(After studying it in silence): Yes. There's no doubt about it. Unless Meade goes to sleep it can only be a question of hours. Lee's a great man, but he can't get out of that.

Making a ring on the map with his finger.

Malins (taking the map again): This ought to be the end, sir.

Grant: Yes. If Lee surrenders, we can all pack up for home.

Malins: By God, sir, it will be splendid, won't it, to be back again?

Grant: By God, sir, it will.

Malins: I beg your pardon, sir.

Grant: You're quite right, Malins. My boy goes away to school next week. Now I may be able to go down with him and see him settled.

DENNIS comes back.

Dennis: Colonel West says, yes, sir, for the last half-hour. The cook says he's sorry, sir. It was a mistake.

Grant: Tell him to keep his mistakes in the kitchen.

Dennis: I will, sir.

He goes back to his place.

Grant (at his papers): Those rifles went up this afternoon?

Malins: Yes, sir.

Another ORDERLY comes in.

Orderly: Mr. Lincoln has just arrived, sir. He's in the yard now.

Grant: All right, I'll come.

THE ORDERLY goes. GRANT rises and crosses to the door, but is met there by LINCOLN and HAY. LINCOLN, in top boots and tall hat that has seen many campaigns, shakes hands with GRANT and takes MALINS'S salute.

Grant: I wasn't expecting you, sir.

Lincoln: No; but I couldn't keep away. How's it going?

They sit.

Grant: Meade sent word an hour and a half ago that Lee was surrounded all but two miles, which was closing in.

Lincoln: That ought about to settle it, eh?

Grant: Unless anything goes wrong in those two miles, sir. I'm expecting a further report from Meade every minute.

Lincoln: Would there be more fighting?

Grant: It will probably mean fighting through the night, more or less. But Lee must realise it's hopeless by the morning.

An Orderly (entering): A despatch, sir.

Grant: Yes.

THE ORDERLY goes, and a YOUNG OFFICER comes in from the field. He salutes and hands a despatch to GRANT.

Officer: From General Meade, sir.

Grant (taking it): Thank you.

He opens it and reads.

You needn't wait.

THE OFFICER salutes and goes.

Yes, they've closed the ring. Meade gives them ten hours. It's timed at eight. That's six o'clock in the morning.

He hands the despatch to LINCOLN.

Lincoln: We must be merciful. Bob Lee has been a gallant fellow.

Grant (taking a paper): Perhaps you'll look through this list, sir. I hope it's the last we shall have.

Lincoln (taking the paper): It's a horrible part of the business, Grant. Any shootings?

Grant: One.

Lincoln: Damn it, Grant, why can't you do without it? No, no, of course not? Who is it?

Grant: Malins.

Malins (opening a book): William Scott, sir. It's rather a hard case.

Lincoln: What is it?

Malins: He had just done a heavy march, sir, and volunteered for double guard duty to relieve a sick friend. He was found asleep at his post.

He shuts the book.

Grant: I was anxious to spare him. But it couldn't be done. It was a critical place, at a gravely critical time.

Lincoln: When is it to be?

Matins: To-morrow, at daybreak, sir.

Lincoln: I don't see that it will do him any good to be shot. Where is he?

Malins: Here, sir.

Lincoln: Can I go and see him?

Grant: Where is he?

Malins: In the barn, I believe, sir.

Grant: Dennis.

Dennis (coming from his table): Yes, sir.

Grant: Ask them to bring Scott in here.

DENNIS goes.

I want to see Colonel West. Malins, ask Templeman if those figures are ready yet.

He goes, and MALINS follows.

Lincoln: Will you, Hay?

HAY goes. After a moment, during which LINCOLN takes the book that MALINS has been reading from, and looks into it, WILLIAM SCOTT is brought in under guard. He is a boy of twenty.

Lincoln (to the GUARD): Thank you. Wait outside, will you?

The MEN salute and withdraw.

Are you William Scott?

Scott: Yes, sir.

Lincoln: You know who I am?

Scott: Yes, sir.

Lincoln: The General tells me you've been court-martialled.

Scott: Yes sir.

Lincoln: Asleep on guard?

Scott: Yes, sir.

Lincoln: It's a very serious offence.

Scott: I know, sir.

Lincoln: What was it?

Scott (a pause): I couldn't keep awake, sir.

Lincoln: You'd had a long march?

Scott: Twenty-three miles, sir.

Lincoln: You were doing double guard?

Scott: Yes, sir.

Lincoln: Who ordered you?

Scott: Well, sir, I offered.

Lincoln: Why?

Scott: Enoch White—he was sick, sir. We come from the same place.

Lincoln: Where's that?

Scott: Vermont, sir.

Lincoln: You live there?

Scott: Yes, sir. My ... we've got a farm down there, sir.

Lincoln: Who has?

Scott: My mother, sir. I've got her photograph, sir.

He takes it from his pocket.

Lincoln (taking it): Does she know about this?

Scott: For God's sake, don't, sir.

Lincoln: There, there, my boy. You're not going to be shot.

Scott (after a pause): Not going to be shot, sir.

Lincoln: No, no.

Scott: Not—going—to—be—shot.

He breaks down, sobbing.

Lincoln (rising and going to him): There, there. I believe you when you tell me that you couldn't keep awake. I'm going to trust you, and send you back to your regiment.

He goes back to his seat.

Scott: When may I go back, sir?

Lincoln: You can go back to-morrow. I expect the fighting will be over, though.

Scott: Is it over yet, sir?

Lincoln: Not quite.

Scott: Please, sir, let me go back to-night—let me go back to-night.

Lincoln: Very well.

He writes.

Do you know where General Meade is?

Scott: No, sir.

Lincoln: Ask one of those men to come here.

SCOTT calls one of his guards in.

Lincoln: Your prisoner is discharged. Take him at once to General Meade with this.

He hands a note to the man.

The Soldier: Yes, sir.

Scott: Thank you, sir.

He salutes and goes out with the SOLDIER.

Lincoln: Hay.

Hay (outside): Yes, sir.

He comes in.

Lincoln: What's the time?

Hay (looking at the watch on the table): Just on half-past nine, sir.

Lincoln: I shall sleep here for a little. You'd better shake down too. They'll wake us if there's any news.

LINCOLN wraps himself up on two chairs.

HAY follows suit on a bench. After a few moments GRANT comes to the door, sees what has happened, blows out the candles quietly, and goes away.

THE CURTAIN FALLS.

The First Chronicler: Under the stars an end is made,

And on the field the Southern blade

Lies broken,

And, where strife was, shall union be,

And, where was bondage, liberty.

The word is spoken....

Night passes.

The Curtain rises on the same scene, LINCOLN and HAY still lying asleep. The light of dawn fills the room. The ORDERLY comes in with two smoking cups of coffee and some biscuits. LINCOLN wakes.

Lincoln: Good-morning.

Orderly: Good-morning, sir.

Lincoln (taking coffee and biscuits): Thank you.

The ORDERLY turns to HAY, who sleeps on, and he hesitates.

Lincoln: Hay. (Shouting.) Hay.

Hay (starting up): Hullo! What the devil is it? I beg your pardon, sir.

Lincoln: Not at all. Take a little coffee.

Hay: Thank you, sir.

He takes coffee and biscuits. The ORDERLY goes.

Lincoln: Slept well, Hay?

Hay: I feel a little crumpled, sir. I think I fell off once.

Lincoln: What's the time?

Hay (looking at the watch): Six o'clock, sir.

GRANT comes in.

Grant: Good-morning, sir; good-morning, Hay.

Lincoln: Good-morning, general.

Hay: Good-morning, sir.

Grant: I didn't disturb you last night. A message has just come from Meade. Lee asked for an armistice at four o'clock.

Lincoln (after a silence): For four years life has been but the hope of this moment. It is strange how simple it is when it comes. Grant, you've served the country very truly. And you've made my work possible.

He takes his hand.

Thank you.

Grant: Had I failed, the fault would not have been yours, sir. I succeeded because you believed in me.

Lincoln: Where is Lee?

Grant: He's coming here. Meade should arrive directly.

Lincoln: Where will Lee wait?

Grant: There's a room ready for him. Will you receive him, sir?

Lincoln: No, no, Grant. That's your affair. You are to mention no political matters. Be generous. But I needn't say that.

Grant (taking a paper from his pocket): Those are the terms I suggest.

Lincoln (reading): Yes, yes. They do you honour.

He places the paper on the table. An ORDERLY comes in.

Orderly: General Meade is here, sir.

Grant: Ask him to come here.

Orderly: Yes, sir.

He goes.

Grant: I learnt a good deal from Robert Lee in early days. He's a better man than most of us. This business will go pretty near the heart, sir.

Lincoln: I'm glad it's to be done by a brave gentleman, Grant.

GENERAL MEADE and CAPTAIN SONE, his aide-de-camp, come in. MEADE salutes. Lincoln: Congratulations, Meade. You've done well.

Meade: Thank you, sir.

Grant: Was there much more fighting?

Meade: Pretty hot for an hour or two.

Grant: How long will Lee be?

Meade: Only a few minutes, I should say, sir.

Grant: You said nothing about terms?

Meade: No, sir.

Lincoln: Did a boy Scott come to you?

Meade: Yes, sir. He went into action at once. He was killed, wasn't he, Sone?

Sone: Yes, sir.

Lincoln: Killed? It's a queer world, Grant.

Meade: Is there any proclamation to be made, sir, about the rebels?

Grant: I—

Lincoln: No, no. I'll have nothing of hanging or shooting these men, even the worst of them. Frighten them out of the country, open the gates, let down the bars, scare them off. Shoo!

He flings out his arms.

Good-bye, Grant. Report at Washington as soon as you can.

He shakes hands with him.

Good-bye, gentlemen. Come along, Hay.

MEADE salutes and LINCOLN goes, followed by HAY.

Grant: Who is with Lee?

Meade: Only one of his staff, sir.

Grant: You might see Malins, will you, Sone, and let us know directly General Lee comes.

Sone: Yes, sir. He goes out.

Grant: Well, Meade, it's been a big job.

Meade: Yes, sir.

Grant: We've had courage and determination. And we've had wits, to beat a great soldier. I'd say that to any man. But it's Abraham Lincoln, Meade, who has kept us a great cause clean to fight for. It does a man's heart good to know he's given victory to such a man to handle. A glass, Meade? (Pouring out whiskey.) No? (Drinking.)

Do you know, Meade, there were fools who wanted me to oppose Lincoln for the next Presidency. I've got my vanities, but I know better than that.

MALINS comes in.

Malins: General Lee is here, sir.

Grant: Meade, will General Lee do me the honour of meeting me here?

MEADE salutes and goes.

Where the deuce is my hat, Malins? And sword.

Malins: Here, sir.

MALINS gets them for him. MEADE and SONE come in, and

stand by the door at attention. ROBERT LEE, General-in-Chief of the Confederate forces, comes in, followed by one of his staff. The days of critical anxiety through which he has just lived have marked themselves on LEE'S face, but his groomed and punctilious toilet contrasts pointedly with GRANT'S unconsidered appearance. The two commanders face each other. GRANT salutes, and LEE replies.

Grant: Sir, you have given me occasion to be proud of my opponent.

Lee: I have not spared my strength. I acknowledge its defeat.

Grant: You have come—

Lee: To ask upon what terms you will accept surrender. Yes.

Grant (taking the paper from the table and handing it to LEE): They are simple. I hope you will not find them ungenerous.

Lee (having read the terms): You are magnanimous, sir. May I make one submission?

Grant: It would be a privilege if I could consider it.

Lee: You allow our officers to keep their horses. That is gracious. Our cavalry troopers' horses also are their own.

Grant: I understand. They will be needed on the farms. It shall be done.

Lee: I thank you. It will do much towards conciliating our people. I accept your terms.

LEE unbuckles his sword, and offers it to GRANT.

Grant: No, no. I should have included that. It has but one rightful place. I beg you.

LEE replaces his sword. GRANT offers his hand and LEE takes it. They salute, and LEE turns to go.

THE CURTAIN FALLS.

The two Chroniclers: A wind blows in the night,

And the pride of the rose is gone.

It laboured, and was delight,

And rains fell, and shone

Suns of the summer days,
And dews washed the bud,
And thanksgiving and praise
Was the rose in our blood.
And out of the night it came,
A wind, and the rose fell,
Shattered its heart of flame,
And how shall June tell
The glory that went with May?
How shall the full year keep
The beauty that ere its day
Was blasted into sleep?
Roses. Oh, heart of man:
Courage, that in the prime
Looked on truth, and began
Conspiracies with time
To flower upon the pain
Of dark and envious earth....
A wind blows, and the brain
Is the dust that was its birth.
What shall the witness cry,
He who has seen alone
With imagination's eye
The darkness overthrown?
Hark: from the long eclipse
The wise words come—
A wind blows, and the lips
Of prophecy are dumb.

SCENE VI.

The evening of April 14, 1865. The small lounge of a theatre. On the far side are the doors of three private boxes. There is silence for a few moments. Then the sound of applause comes from the auditorium beyond. The box doors are opened. In the centre box can be seen LINCOLN and STANTON, MRS. LINCOLN, another lady, and an officer, talking together.

The occupants come out from the other boxes into the lounge, where small knots of people have gathered from different directions, and stand or sit talking busily.

A Lady: Very amusing, don't you think?

Her Companion: Oh, yes. But it's hardly true to life, is it?

Another Lady: Isn't that dark girl clever? What's her name?

A Gentleman (consulting his programme:) Eleanor Crowne.

Another Gentleman: There's a terrible draught, isn't there? I shall have a stiff neck.

His Wife: You should keep your scarf on.

The Gentleman: It looks so odd.

Another Lady: The President looks very happy this evening, doesn't he?

Another: No wonder, is it? He must be a proud man.

A young man, dressed in black, passes among the people, glancing furtively into LINCOLN'S box, and disappears. It is JOHN WILKES BOOTH.

A Lady (greeting another): Ah, Mrs. Bennington. When do you expect your husband back?

They drift away. SUSAN, carrying cloaks and wraps, comes in. She goes to the box, and speaks to MRS. LINCOLN. Then she comes away, and sits down apart from the crowd to wait.

A Young Man: I rather think of going on the stage myself. My friends tell me I'm uncommon good. Only I don't think my health would stand it.

A Girl: Oh, it must be a very easy life. Just acting—that's easy enough.

A cry of "Lincoln" comes through the auditorium. It is taken up, with shouts of "The President," "Speech," "Abraham Lincoln," "Father Abraham," and so on. The conversation in the lounge stops as the talkers turn to listen. After a few moments, LINCOLN is seen to rise. There is a burst of cheering. The people in the lounge stand round the box door. LINCOLN holds up his hand, and there is a sudden silence.

Lincoln: My friends, I am touched, deeply touched, by this mark of your good-will. After four dark and difficult years, we have achieved the great purpose for which we set out. General Lee's surrender to General Grant leaves but one Confederate force in the field, and the end is immediate and certain. (Cheers.) I have but little to say at this moment. I claim not to have controlled events, but confess plainly that events have controlled me. But as events have come before me, I have seen them always with one faith. We have preserved the American Union, and we have abolished a great wrong. (Cheers.) The task of reconciliation, of setting order where there is now confusion, of bringing about a settlement at once just and merciful, and of directing the life of a reunited country into prosperous channels of good-will and generosity, will demand all our wisdom, all our loyalty. It is the proudest hope of my life that I may be of some service in this work. (Cheers.) Whatever it may be, it can be but little in return for all the kindness and forbearance that I have received. With malice toward none, with charity for all, it is for us to resolve that this nation, under God, shall have a new birth of freedom; and that government of the people, by the people, for the people, shall not perish from the earth.

There is a great sound of cheering. It dies down, and a boy passes through the lounge and calls out "Last act, ladies and gentlemen." The people disperse, and the box doors are closed. SUSAN is left alone and there is silence.

After a few moments, BOOTH appears. He watches SUSAN and sees that her gaze is fixed away from him. He creeps along to the centre box and disengages a hand from under his cloak. It holds a revolver. Poising himself, he opens the door with a swift movement, fires, flings the door to again, and rushes away. The door is thrown open again, and the OFFICER follows in pursuit. Inside the box, MRS. LINCOLN is kneeling by her husband, who is supported by STANTON. A DOCTOR runs across the lounge and goes into the box. There is complete silence in the theatre. The door closes again.

Susan (who has run to the box door, and is kneeling there, sobbing): Master, master! No, no, not my master!

The other box doors have opened, and the occupants with others have collected in little terror-struck groups in the lounge. Then the centre door opens, and STANTON comes out, closing it behind him.

Stanton: Now he belongs to the ages.

THE CHRONICLERS speak.

First Chronicler: Events go by. And upon circumstance Disaster strikes with the blind sweep of chance. And this our mimic action was a theme, Kinsmen, as life is, clouded as a dream.

Second Chronicler: But, as we spoke, presiding everywhere Upon event was one man's character. And that endures; it is the token sent Always to man for man's own government.

THE CURTAIN FALLS.

❏❏❏❏